BEING WOKE

Social Awareness or Political Overcorrection?

by Kate Conley

© 2024 ReferencePoint Press, Inc.
Printed in the United States

For more information, contact:
ReferencePoint Press, Inc.
PO Box 27779
San Diego, CA 92198
www.ReferencePointPress.com

ALL RIGHTS RESERVED.

No part of this work covered by the copyright hereon may be reproduced or used in any form or by any means—graphic, electronic, or mechanical, including photocopying, recording, taping, web distribution, or information storage retrieval systems—without the written permission of the publisher.

LIBRARY OF CONGRESS CATALOGING-IN-PUBLICATION DATA

Names: Conley, Kate A., 1977- author.
Title: Being woke: social awareness or political overcorrection? / by Kate Conley.
Description: San Diego, CA: ReferencePoint Press, Inc., [2024] | Includes bibliographical references and index. | Audience: Ages 15–18 years | Audience: Grades 10–12
Identifiers: LCCN 2023009809 (print) | LCCN C (eBook) | ISBN 9781678205621 (hardcover) | ISBN 9781678205638 (eBook)
Subjects: LCSH: Education--Political aspects--United States. | Intersectionality (Sociology)--Political aspects--United States. | Conservatism--United States--21st century. | Liberalism--United States--21st century. | Online social networks--Political aspects--United States. | Internet and activism--United States. | Political correctness--United States. | Cancel culture--United States. | Culture conflict--United States.
Classification: LCC LC89 .C64 2024 (print) | LCC LC89 (eBook) | DDC 306.430973--dc23/eng/20230313
LC record available at https://lccn.loc.gov/2023009809
LC ebook record available at https://lccn.loc.gov/2023009810

CONTENTS

INTRODUCTION — 4
   MAKING HISTORY OR DEFILING IT?

CHAPTER ONE — 8
   THE ORIGINS OF WOKE

CHAPTER TWO — 20
   BEING WOKE

CHAPTER THREE — 32
   "WHERE WOKE GOES TO DIE"

CHAPTER FOUR — 46
   LIFE IN A WOKE NATION

Source Notes	58
For Further Research	60
Index	62
Image Credits	64
About the Author	64

INTRODUCTION

Making History or Defiling It?

The pop star and classically trained flutist Lizzo received a one-of-a-kind invitation while on tour in the fall of 2022. Carla Hayden, the head of the Library of Congress, invited Lizzo to the library's flute vault. The vault has more than 1,000 flutes in its collection, including a crystal flute from 1813 that belonged to President James Madison. Wasting little time, Lizzo accepted Hayden's invitation. When Lizzo arrived at the Library of Congress in Washington, DC, a few days later, the curator of the flute collection, Carol Lynn Ward-Bamford, provided her with an opportunity to play several of the instruments. The library then granted Lizzo permission to play Madison's flute at her Washington, DC, concert.

At the concert, Ward-Bamford joined Lizzo on stage with the historic flute. Before taking the instrument, Lizzo pumped up the crowd. Then she raised the delicate instrument to her lips, and its rich tones filled the auditorium. Now warmed up, Lizzo played a trill on the flute while twerking. This sexually suggestive dance move is liked by some people and hated by others. The crowd erupted in applause.

With an awestruck look on her face, Lizzo raised the flute above her head and then gave it back to Ward-Bamford. The entire flute performance had lasted less than ninety seconds, yet it kindled a controversy that reverberated across the media. At its center was a much-debated idea gripping the nation: being woke.

Lizzo has played the flute since age ten. When she visited the Library of Congress in 2022, she got to play James Madison's flute.

A Variety of Responses

The word *woke* means different things to different people. For some, it's an awareness of social injustices in society. For others, it's a disparaging way to describe radical liberal viewpoints. The response to Lizzo's flute performance showed the wide range of these differing views.

Many people praised the performance. Concert attendee Carrie Arnold said, "It's not often you see a founding father's personal artifacts reclaimed as a symbol of pop culture and a celebration [of] Black female empowerment."[1] Reclaiming the past had more to do with the

> "It's not often you see a founding father's personal artifacts reclaimed as a symbol of pop culture and a celebration [of] Black female empowerment."
> —Carrie Arnold, Lizzo concert attendee

flute's owner than the instrument itself. Madison was an important figure in the nation's founding, but he enslaved people. A Black woman like Lizzo likely would not have been allowed to play this priceless flute in Madison's era. Yet more than 200 years later, Lizzo was doing just that in front of a packed stadium. For some people, this was a symbol of how much society had progressed since the nation's founding.

Not everyone thought Lizzo's performance was historic, however. Candance Owens, a prominent conservative commentator, found the entire display offensive. "She's not making history here," Owens said of Lizzo's performance. "She's defiling history. It's like spraying graffiti on a historical building and going, 'Oh, it's art.' No. It's not art. We're not going to call it art. We're not going to call it making history."[2] Pushing the idea even further, conservative media pundit Matt Walsh said, "Lizzo playing James Madison's flute was a form of racial retribution, according to the woke Left."[3]

For Owens and Walsh, the problem was not that Lizzo had played a priceless, historic relic. It was how she did it that offended them. Rather than being dressed in a dignified evening gown in a traditional concert hall, Lizzo wore a sequined body suit with her buttocks bared. Adding to the offense, she twerked while playing the flute.

The Culture Wars

The wildly differing responses to a performance that lasted less than two minutes highlighted the cultural unrest across the United States. In the media, this unrest is frequently referred to as the culture wars. On one side of the battlefield are people who want to conserve the traditional values the country was founded upon. On the other side are people who believe that greater equality for historically marginalized groups requires changes to society.

Both sides are vocal, and the way they speak about their positions has given rise to a collection of buzzwords, including *cancel culture*, *white privilege*, and *critical race theory*. None of these terms, however, have garnered quite as much attention, hatred, or admiration as the word *woke*. What began as a word of

> "Lizzo playing James Madison's flute was a form of racial retribution, according to the woke Left."
>
> —Matt Walsh, conservative media pundit

empowerment in Black culture has morphed into a catchall word representing the division in the nation today.

People often use social media to call out others who think differently from them. They may try to shame other people for their viewpoints.

CHAPTER ONE

The Origins of Woke

Looking relaxed in a striped button-down shirt and sport coat, former president Barack Obama joined several youth leaders at an Obama Foundation meeting in October 2019. The foundation seeks to inspire, empower, and connect people to improve their communities. The meeting was held in Chicago, Illinois, and brought together leaders from across the globe. While the conversation was wide ranging, it was Obama's comments on woke culture that spread quickly online. He questioned young people who used "being woke" as part of their identity, urging them to see others in a more nuanced way rather than being all good or all bad. "This idea of purity and you're never compromised, and you're always politically 'woke' and all that stuff," said Obama. "You should get over that quickly. The world is messy; there are ambiguities. People who do really good stuff have flaws."[4]

    Obama was not discouraging young activists from calling out social injustices when they saw them. Instead, he was pushing them to rethink their activism. He wanted them to have a broader perspective than simply judging people for not being woke and canceling them, which is a form of boycotting a person. "Like, if I tweet or hashtag about how you didn't do something right or used the wrong verb, then I can sit back and feel pretty good about myself, cause, 'Man, you see how woke I was, I called you out,'" said Obama. "That's not activism. That's not bringing about change. If all you're doing is casting stones, you're probably not going to get that far. That's easy to do."[5]

Barack Obama was president from 2009 to 2017. He created the Obama Foundation in 2014.

    Being woke rose to prominence in US politics and culture in the 2020s. The word *woke* was not new, however. Black communities have used the terms *wake up*, *stay woke,* and *be woke* to highlight racial and social injustices for more than a century. In 1904, for example, a newspaper called the *Baltimore Afro-American* printed an editorial urging readers to wake up regarding voting rights. A 1912 article in the *Chicago Defender*, which was the nation's most influential weekly Black newspaper, pushed for greater racial activism under the headline "Race in Chicago Must Wake Up!" Then in the 1920s, Black social activist Marcus Garvey urged Black communities in the United States and across the globe to have a greater political awareness. His rallying cry was "Wake up Ethiopia! Wake up Africa!"[6]

Huddie "Lead Belly" Ledbetter was inducted into the Blues Hall of Fame and the Rock and Roll Hall of Fame in the 1980s. His music inspired many musicians.

A few years later, the concept appeared again, this time in a song by blues musician Huddie "Lead Belly" Ledbetter. In 1938, he recorded a song called "Scottsboro Boys." It was about the arrest and trial of nine young Black men in Scottsboro, Alabama, in 1931. The young men had been wrongfully convicted of raping two white women, resulting in a public outcry. At the end of the recording, Lead Belly gives a brief interview. "I made this little song about down there," he said, referring to Alabama. "I advise everybody to be a little careful when they go down there. Stay woke. Keep your eyes open."[7]

In the years following the song, Lead Belly's use of *woke* to mean being alert to racially motived dangers grew in Black communities. The term first gained mainstream attention in 1962, when novelist William Melvin Kelley wrote an opinion piece in the *New York Times* titled "If You're Woke, You Dig It." The article examined how white communities frequently appropriate words that originate in Black communities, such as *cool*, *chick*, and *woke*. In this process, the meaning of the words often changes. While Kelley didn't realize it at the time, this is exactly what would happen to the word *woke* more than fifty years after his article first appeared.

> "*Woke* in its initial inception meant political consciousness for Black people about the histories of anti-Blackness in this country and globally, rather than this more generalized kind of political consciousness that it came to take up [today]."
>
> —Deandre Miles-Hercules, linguist

Aside from the Kelley article, the word *woke* in this sense remained mostly limited to the Black community for the next several decades. Deandre Miles-Hercules, a linguist at the University of California-Santa Barbara, explained what this term meant among people in Black communities during this period. She said, "*Woke* in its initial inception meant political consciousness for Black people about the histories of anti-Blackness in this country and globally,

Malcolm X was a civil rights activist. His speeches drew large crowds.

rather than this more generalized kind of political consciousness that it came to take up [today].[8]

Wokeness in Black Communities

During the 1960s, the term *woke* continued to be used among civil rights leaders. One of those leaders, Malcolm X, gave a well-known speech in April 1964 called "The Ballot or the Bullet." In it, he accused white politicians of manipulating Black voters. Like Garvey before him, Malcolm X urged fellow Black citizens to become aware of the situation. "So it's time in 1964 to wake up," he said. "They get all the Negro vote, and after they get it, the Negro gets nothing in return. All they did when they got to Washington was give a few big Negroes big jobs. Those big Negroes didn't need big jobs, they already had jobs. That's camouflage, that's trickery, that's treachery, window-dressing."[9]

Just three months after Malcolm X's speech, the Civil Rights Act became law in the United States. It outlawed discrimination based on race, color, religion, sex, national origin, disability, or age. This was the broadest, most revolutionary civil rights legislation passed since the Reconstruction Era after the Civil War (1861–1865). In June 1965, less than a year after the act became law, Dr. Martin Luther King Jr. gave a commencement speech at Oberlin College. His speech, entitled "Remaining Awake Through a Great Revolution," challenged graduates to remain awake to social injustices that remained and seek peaceful ways to remedy them.

Arising out of the civil rights era was a musical group called the Last Poets. Its music, which united spoken word poetry and music, focused on Black reawakening. The music the Last Poets created is often considered the forerunner of modern rap. Like Lead Belly before them, the group recorded a song calling for Black people to raise their consciousness. In 1970, the group recorded a song called "Wake Up, N––." It was a stinging reality check and a call to action for people within Black communities.

Two years later, playwright Barry Beckham created a biographical work about Garvey's life, called *Garvey Lives!* In the play, one character says, "I been sleeping all my life. And now that Mr. Garvey done woke me up, I'm gon stay woke. And I'm gon help him wake up other Black folk."[10] The concept appeared again in Spike Lee's 1988 movie *School Daze*. Set at a historically Black college, the movie has a scene where one of the lead characters, played by Laurence Fishburne, spends several minutes urging fellow students to wake up and unite as Black people.

While the references to waking up and being woke spanned a variety of settings—civil rights speeches, early rap music, plays, and movies—they remained firmly rooted in Black culture. Aside from Kelley's *New York Times* article in the early 1960s, the term *woke* stayed under the radar of white mainstream media and culture for decades.

Woke Goes Mainstream

The idea of being woke reached a wider audience in 2008, when Grammy-winning musician Erykah Badu released a song called "Master Teacher." A chance meeting between Badu and musician Georgia Anne Muldrow inspired the song. Muldrow had written

BLM grew into a massive social movement. Some polls found that between 15 million and 26 million people participated in BLM demonstrations in the summer of 2020.

"Master Teacher," which was a track on an unreleased album she had recorded. In the song, Muldrow referenced being woke in three different ways: being physically awake, suspecting a partner of cheating, and being aware of racial injustice.

Muldrow's track inspired Badu, and the two musicians collaborated on an altered version of the song. It was released on Badu's album *New Amerykah Part One*. The song uses all three meanings of the word, with the refrain repeating the phrase "I stay woke." The song's impact on spreading the concept of wokeness is hard to overstate. "The refrain revitalized the pro-black meaning of the word *woke* . . . for a new generation," said journalist Jonah E. Bromwich in an article for *Vulture*, which marked the album's tenth anniversary.[11]

Badu's song spread the concept of wokeness further than in the past, yet it would take the intersection of two other things—social media and violence against unarmed Black people—to fully push the idea into mainstream US culture.

On February 26, 2012, George Zimmerman was volunteering as a neighborhood watchman in Sanford, Florida. He spotted a Black seventeen-year-old named Trayvon Martin, who was walking back from a convenience store after buying candy. Zimmerman called 911 to report Martin as suspicious. The 911 dispatcher told Zimmerman not to approach Martin. Soon after, a scuffle between the two occurred, and gunshots rang out. Zimmerman admitted to shooting and killing Martin. He said it was in self-defense.

Zimmerman was charged with murder, but on July 13, 2013, a jury found him not guilty. The verdict spurred outrage, not just in Florida but across the nation. Martin had been unarmed at the time of the shooting. People raised questions about how his race may have impacted Zimmerman's decision to shoot and the jury's not-guilty verdict. Protesters assembled in cities across the country to express their anger. Response to the verdict also inspired the creation of Black Lives Matter (BLM), a group dedicated to ending acts of violence against Black people. BLM organized on Twitter using the hashtag #StayWoke.

Black Twitter

The rise of *woke* in mainstream society was in large part thanks to Black Twitter. This is a large network of people whose use Twitter to spread awareness about issues important to Black communities. According to writer J. A. Parham, "Black Twitter has become the most dynamic subset not only of Twitter but of the wider social internet. Capable of creating, shaping, and remixing popular culture at light speed, it remains the incubator of nearly every meme . . . hashtag . . . and social justice cause . . . worth knowing about. It is both news and analysis, call and response, judge and jury—a comedy showcase, therapy session, and family cookout all in one. Black Twitter is a multiverse, simultaneously an archive and an all-seeing lens into the future."

Jason Parham, "A People's History of Black Twitter, Part I," *Wired*, July 15, 2021. www.wired.com.

Though BLM was growing, it did not yet receive significant coverage by the mainstream media. Then a shooting took place in Ferguson, Missouri, on August 9, 2014, that would change everything. On that day, an eighteen-year-old Black man named Michael Brown and a friend were walking down a street. They were stopped by a white police officer. After an altercation, the police officer fired at Brown and killed him. Brown was unarmed at the time.

> "Stay woke just means pay attention to everything, don't lean on your own understanding or anyone else's, observe, evolve, eliminate things that no longer evolve."
> —Erykah Badu, Grammy-winning musician

The shooting sparked a city-wide protest over police brutality and racial profiling. News of the Ferguson protests spread on social media platforms. These platforms allowed Ferguson residents to share information with each other quickly. They also provided a megaphone to share news of the protests across the country in real time. As coverage of the events spread, two hashtags began to trend across Twitter: #BlackLivesMatter and #StayWoke.

André Brock is a professor of Black digital studies at the Georgia Institute of Technology. He studied the connection between social media platforms such as Twitter and the spread of the woke ideology. At the time, Twitter limited its users to posts with 140 characters. Words like *BLM* and *woke* had only three and four characters, so they became an efficient shorthand to mention complex ideas about race on Twitter. Their usefulness also showed how the influence of Twitter users could be harnessed in a new way. Up until that point, the platform had largely been relegated to socializing. As the platform evolved, people realized it had the power to reach millions of users in a short time. Because of this, it could be a significant tool for social activism.

The Ferguson protests and social media had ushered the hashtag #StayWoke into the national spotlight. *Woke*'s long, winding path from Marcus Garvey to Michael Brown was far from complete, however. The meaning of *woke*, a word that had once been a signal of solidarity and unity against race-based dangers and injustices, was about to change in ways few Americans could foresee.

An Expanding Definition

People's use of *woke* gradually increased. The term was used in new settings and by new groups after social media drew attention to Brown's death. "I would argue that a lot of white people started catching on after 2014 or 2015," said Damariyé L. Smith, a professor of Contemporary Black/African American Rhetoric and Media Studies at San Diego State University. "From there, you start having a lot of other white folks . . . start using the terminology like, 'I'm woke, I'm white, but I'm woke.'"[12]

As the number of people who used the word *woke* expanded, its meaning began to change. Some groups adopted *woke* to bring awareness to their own causes, modifying its original meaning in the process. Others saw it as the newest hip term to add to their vocabularies. In early 2016, MTV included *woke* on a list of ten slang words everyone should know. The word gradually became synonymous with political awareness and progressive ideology.

For example, at the Women's March in Washington, DC, held in January 2017 to protest the inauguration of President Donald Trump, the word *woke* appeared on many signs. Children who

Pejoration

Language is always changing. Sometimes the meanings of words also change. Linguists are people who study language. They use the term *pejoration* to describe one way a word's meaning can change over time. Pejoration is a process that occurs when a word takes on a new meaning that is negative or less favorable than its original one. The word *woke* has undergone pejoration. Its original meaning was to be aware of racial oppression. Later, it became a rallying cry against police brutality. In the 2020s, it was a catchall term for nearly anything related to race or a progressive agenda.

joined their mothers at the march carried signs that said things like "I [Heart] Naps But I Stay Woke." One toddler at the march held a sign filled with marker scribbles. Her picture was shared thousands of times on social media along with the hashtag #WokeBaby.

As the word's use expanded, liberals and conservatives had a hard time agreeing on what the term meant. When asked about its meaning in 2019, Badu explained, "Stay woke just means pay attention to everything, don't lean on your own understanding or anyone else's, observe, evolve, eliminate things that no longer evolve. That's what it means. Stay conscious, stay awake. It doesn't mean judge others. It doesn't mean gang up on somebody who you feel is not woke. That's not evolved."[13]

Some conservatives disagreed with definitions like the one Badu put forward. Instead, they saw *woke* as less about increased social awareness and more about pushing a progressive agenda. "The woke regime rests primarily on a charge that racial evil was systemically and deliberately embedded long ago, by the white patriarchy, in the heart of American life, and that this ugliness thrives undiminished," wrote *Wall Street Journal* columnist Peggy Noonan in an article that condemned wokeism.[14]

Debates about the meaning of *woke* became more complex by mid-2021. Around that time, *woke* began appearing more frequently in speeches and tweets by Republicans. They used it to show contempt for any perceived liberal ideas. In 2020, for example, Aunt Jemima syrup and Uncle Ben's rice were ridiculed for being woke when they rebranded their traditional logos, which had promoted racial stereotypes.

> "The woke regime rests primarily on a charge that racial evil was systemically and deliberately embedded long ago, by the white patriarchy, in the heart of American life, and that this ugliness thrives undiminished."
> —Peggy Noonan, conservative columnist

The term **woke** catapulted into the mainstream in the 2010s. It helped make some people more aware of social injustices.

CHAPTER TWO

Being Woke

On the evening of May 25, 2020, police officers in Minneapolis, Minnesota, responded to a call about a person trying to use a possible counterfeit twenty-dollar bill. When officers arrived, they encountered the suspect, a 46-year-old Black man named George Floyd. A struggled ensued, and Floyd

Toppling Statues

In the weeks after George Floyd's death, protesters pushed for the removal of some statues that glorified people from America's past. Confederate statues honor men who fought against the United States in the Civil War in order to preserve the practice of slavery. For many people, they symbolize the nation's legacy of racism. The situation is similar with statues of colonial leaders, who may be seen to stand for Native American genocide and racial oppression. Some statues have been removed because of this, but many still stand. They have become lighting rods for protesters as they seek to draw attention to the nation's racial injustices.

In several cities, protesters vandalized and toppled the statues. Some city and state leaders began to take down the statues as a result. What to do with these massive statues has been a problem for local leaders, many of whom have opted to place them in storage. "Putting [the statues] in quarantine for a period of years is a fine solution for now," said Sheffield Hale, leader of the Atlanta History Center. "Maybe they can be brought out of quarantine a decade or two or three later and we can have a conversation about them. But for now, they're so toxic."

Will Wright, "Cities Want to Remove Toxic Monuments. But Who Will Take Them?" New York Times, *June 23, 2020. www.nytimes.com.*

George Floyd's murder received international attention. Millions of people took to the streets to protest police brutality.

ended up handcuffed and facedown on the ground. A white police officer named Derek Chauvin helped pin Floyd to the ground, pressing his knee on Floyd's neck. Chauvin held this position for more than nine minutes. Floyd repeatedly said, "I can't breathe," but Chauvin did not release him.[15] During this time, Floyd became unresponsive and was later pronounced dead.

A seventeen-year-old girl named Darnella Frazier recorded Floyd's arrest and struggle with Chauvin. She posted her video online and it went viral, being shared and reshared countless times on social media platforms. As Frazier's video spread, it sparked outrage that had been building in the Black communities of Minneapolis for decades. Protesters demanded justice not only for Floyd but for all the people of color who had been victims of police brutality. A day after the incident, protesters met at the site where Floyd had died, carrying signs that read "I can't breathe." Then they went to a nearby police station, where they damaged the building and a squad car. Protests lasted for days in Minneapolis, with some evolving into rioting and looting.

The situation in Minneapolis was tense, but it was far from unusual. Across the nation, news of Floyd's death sparked hundreds of protests throughout the summer of 2020. It ultimately led to what many experts described as a racial reckoning. This reckoning forced into the mainstream topics that had largely been glossed over in the past, such as why Black people are nearly three times more likely to die at the hands of police than white people. It also forced Americans to face uncomfortable parts of history, such as why Founding Fathers who owned enslaved people are still respected today.

> "Stay woke. Don't just open your eyes, stretch, yawn, and think that it's over. No, stay woke. Now that your eyes are open and you know what my culture goes through, I want my culture to stay woke, but I want the other cultures that's supporting us to stay woke. To keep this movement flourishing, to keep my brother's name ringing in the ears of everyone."
> —Terrence Floyd, speaking on the one-year anniversary of his brother George Floyd's death

A year after Floyd's death, his brother Terrence commented on the impact it had made not only on his family but on the whole nation. "Stay woke. Don't just open your eyes, stretch, yawn, and think that it's over," he told a group of people assembled in Brooklyn, New York, to mark the one-year anniversary of his brother's death. "No, stay woke. Now that your eyes are open and you know what my culture goes through, I want my culture to stay woke, but I want the other cultures that's supporting us to stay woke. To keep this movement flourishing, to keep my brother's name ringing in the ears of everyone."[16]

Reframing History and Race

For Terrence Floyd and millions of other Americans, being woke is more than just a hashtag or a trendy slang term. It has evolved into an identity with a strong political connection. Those who are labeled woke—either by themselves or others—typically hold liberal political viewpoints. In a July 2021 poll of registered voters, 60 percent of Democrats viewed being woke as a positive thing and 70 percent of them said wokeness was helping move the country in a good direction. In contrast, only 20 percent of Republicans said being woke was good and 72 percent said wokeness was causing unrest and fueling differences between people.

One of the biggest sources of social and political unrest centers on race. Most Americans agree that racism is bad—that in itself is not a woke position. Yet the way people frame it differs greatly based on their age, education level, political affiliation, and race. According to a 2022 Pew Research Poll, for example, 77 percent of Black Americans favor giving reparations to descendants of enslaved people. Reparations are a way to correct a past wrong. They could take the form of cash payments, scholarships, or financial aid to buy a home or start a business. Some people believe reparations would address the wealth gap that exists between Black and white Americans. Much of the gap can be traced back to racist practices in the past. Jim Crow segregation laws, discriminatory housing policies called redlining, and many other anti-Black practices have hindered many Black people from building wealth like their white counterparts.

Not everyone sees reparations as a solution to the wealth gap, however. Only 18 percent of white respondents in the Pew poll favored reparations. Some of them may point to the idea that the United States is a meritocracy. In a meritocracy, everyone has an equal, fair chance at success if they work hard. It ignores how other factors—such as race or generational wealth—impact success and opportunities. In a meritocracy, success is attributed to skill and hard work alone. Under this viewpoint, the wealth gap results from a lack of hard work or skill, not complex social factors.

Differences in viewpoints about race also appear when it comes to how the nation's history is framed. Most Americans agree that learning about the challenging parts of the nation's history, such as slavery, is important. Not everyone agrees on how it

In January 2023, The 1619 Project *was turned into a TV documentary. Nikole Hannah-Jones attended the premiere.*

should be done, though. Some people believe that the past, while useful and important to learn from, should not determine today's social policies. They argue that focusing on the past deepens divisions among people today. Others argue that Americans must acknowledge the past and see how it continues to influence the nation. Without doing that, the experiences of marginalized groups may be overlooked.

Perhaps no piece of writing has stirred more controversy on the topics of race and history than "The 1619 Project." This collection of essays first appeared in the *New York Times Magazine* in 2019. Its publication marked the 400th anniversary of the arrival of the first ship of enslaved people in the American colonies. The project sought to show the nation's history through the lens of Black Americans, including the lasting effects of slavery and the many contributions of Black people. Nikole Hannah-Jones, editor of "The 1619 Project," believes looking at history through this lens can enlighten Americans about the present. She wants to show people that historical injustices still have an impact on people today.

The project also directly challenged some of the ideals the nation was founded upon. "What many people don't know, and I point this out in my essay, is that one of the reasons we even decided to become a nation in the first place is over the issue of slavery," said Hannah-Jones. "One of the reasons that the founders wanted to break off from Britain is they were afraid that Britain was going to begin regulating slavery and maybe even moving towards abolishment. And we were making so much money off of slavery that the founders wanted to be able to continue it."[17]

The 1776 Commission

Unhappy with the woke ideas in the "The 1619 Project," President Donald Trump responded by launching his own US history project: The 1776 Commission. Trump hoped it would "restore patriotic education to our schools." While announcing the commission in 2020, he said, "Our mission is to defend the legacy of America's founding, the virtue of America's heroes, and the nobility of the American character. We must clear away the twisted web of lies in our schools and classrooms and teach our children the magnificent truth about our country."[1]

The eighteen-member commission Trump appointed got to work quickly. It released its report on January 18, 2021, just days before Trump left the White House. Upon its publication, the report was fiercely criticized by historians for its bias and factual errors. One of those historians was James Grossman, director of the American Historical Association. "It's a hack job. It's not a work of history," Grossman said. "It's a work of contentious politics designed to stoke culture wars."[2] On his first day in office, January 20, 2021, President Joe Biden disbanded the commission.

[1] *"Teaching Our Children,"* C-SPAN, *September 17, 2020.* www.c-span.org.
[2] *Gillian Brockell, "'A Hack Job,' 'Outright Lies': Trump Commission's '1776 Report' Outrages Historians,"* Washington Post, *January 19, 2021.* www.washingtonpost.com.

Not everyone agreed with Hannah-Jones, and some historians took issue with the accuracy of her claims. When some schools began to use "The 1619 Project" as part of their history curriculum, the discourse around it grew divisive. Critics claimed the project rewrote history by prioritizing the narrative of slavery, which served to indoctrinate students with woke, liberal political viewpoints. "['The 1619 Project'] engages students, and it makes them activists, which is what a lot of teachers want to do," said Mary Graber, author of *Debunking the 1619 Project*. "There are way too many woke teachers. They've been trained in colleges of education to produce not knowledgeable citizens, but left-wing social activists."[18]

> "['The 1619 Project'] engages students, and it makes them activists, which is what a lot of teachers want to do. There are way too many woke teachers. They've been trained in colleges of education to produce not knowledgeable citizens, but left-wing social activists."
> —Mary Graber, author of *Debunking the 1619 Project*

Other critics claimed that not only was "The 1619 Project" full of historical errors, it also belittled the ideals of the nation's founding. Peter Wood, author of *1620: A Critical Response to the 1619 Project*, argued that the project's premise was an unfair look at history by biased authors. "'The 1619 Project' is, arguably, part of a larger effort to destroy America by people who find it unbearably bad," said Wood. "The project treats the founding principles of our nation as an illusion—a contemptible illusion. In their place is a single idea: that America was founded on racist exploitation."[19]

Wokeness Expands

While awareness of racial injustices remains at the historical heart of being woke, the concept has expanded. It now includes looking at how other traits—such as gender, sexuality, and class—affect the way Americans are treated within society. Looking at these traits in combination is referred to as intersectionality. Civil rights activist and legal scholar Kimberlé Crenshaw coined the term *intersectionality* in 1989. She used it to explain how traits including race and sex intersect and overlap to affect a person's experiences.

Originally Crenshaw's ideas about intersectionality centered on women of color and their experiences with the legal system. As the term became more mainstream, however, people began to apply it to a variety of identities. "Intersectionality is a lens through which you can see where power comes and collides, where it interlocks and intersects," said Crenshaw in a 2017 interview with Columbia University Law School. "It's not simply that there's a race problem here, a gender problem here, and a class or LBGTQ problem there. Many times that framework erases what happens to people who are subject to all of these things."[20]

Crenshaw gives the example of looking at income through the lens of intersectionality. Though gains have been made over the years, statistics show that many women still receive less in wages over their lifetimes than men. When parenthood intersects with sex, women face a greater financial loss than men. Add race into the mix and wage inequality becomes even more noticeable. Statistically speaking, a Black woman who is a parent is likely to have less financial security than a white man who is a parent. The intersection of race, sex, and parenthood combine to create very different experiences for each person.

> "Intersectionality is a lens through which you can see where power comes and collides, where it interlocks and intersects. It's not simply that there's a race problem here, a gender problem here, and a class or LBGTQ problem there. Many times that framework erases what happens to people who are subject to all of these things."
> —Kimberlé Crenshaw, civil rights activist and legal scholar

"Intersectionality is simply about how certain aspects of who you are will increase your access to the good things or your exposure to the bad things in life. Like many other social-justice ideas, it stands because it resonates with people's lives, but because it resonates with people's lives, it's under attack," said Crenshaw. "There's nothing new about defenders of the status quo criticizing those who are demanding that injustices be addressed. It's all a crisis over a sense that things might actually have to change for equality to be real."[21]

Critics have a different take on intersectionality. They argue that it creates a hierarchy of victims. The more oppressed groups a person can claim membership in, the closer to the top of the

The LGBTQ+ community has historically faced a lot of discrimination. People who are LGBTQ+ face higher rates of violence than people who are not part of this community.

hierarchy they land. So a white woman would, for example, belong to one oppressed group—women. By this same logic, a Black woman would belong to two groups—women and people of color—and thus have a more elevated place on the hierarchy. A Black woman who is also a lesbian would be higher still, because she would belong to three groups—women, people of color, and the LGBTQ+ community. Historically, most of the nation's institutions have been created for and based upon the values of straight white men. As a result, they face the least oppression and sit at the bottom of such a hierarchy.

Intersectionality empowers each group to speak about its experience with authority. For an issue like gay marriage, for example, members of the LGBTQ+ community would share their expertise and experiences. Other groups would support them as allies, though they would not speak on their behalf. In addition, when an issue like abortion is discussed, women's groups would have the privilege to speak while other groups serve as their allies. The problem with this setup, according to critics, is that it censors anyone who is not part of the affected group. One of the biggest complaints about intersectionality is this focus on a person's in-group experiences.

"The sort of tribal politics that we are seeing, and that I think does in some ways escalate toward violence, is a politics where we say, 'You cannot have a discussion with me because you have not had my experiences,'" said conservative pundit Ben Shapiro. "The intersectional politics of the United States is really dangerous and it's not just on the left side of the aisle. It's on the right side of the aisle, as well."[22]

Diversity, Equity, and Inclusion

In 2020, many businesses reassessed what kinds of bias and discrimination existed in their organizations. Many workplaces revamped their Diversity, Equity, and Inclusion (DEI) practices. DEI is a framework used to ensure that employees—especially those who are traditionally marginalized—are treated fairly. In 2020, hiring of DEI experts tripled, and companies paid $3.4 billion to outside DEI training firms.

At its most basic level, DEI is an intentional focus on each of the three elements in its name. Diversity in a workplace means embracing and prioritizing the need for employees with different backgrounds. Businesses with employees who have differing races, genders, sexualities, religions, and nationalities have diversity. Equity acknowledges that not all employees are starting from a level playing field. It is a focus on making sure all employees have the opportunities and resources they need to succeed. Inclusion means making sure employees of diverse backgrounds feel welcomed, respected, and valued.

The way workplaces implement these values varies greatly. For example, a company may work to improve the way it supports diverse gender identities. This could include adding health benefits for someone transitioning or updating the language in corporate policies to make it more inclusive for members of the LGBTQ+ community. Another example is to provide training that raises awareness of issues such as unconscious bias, which is a stereotype or false belief about a group that an individual may hold without realizing it. Other initiatives may focus on improving mental health, creating multigenerational teams, and building a diverse management group.

Supporters of DEI applauded these efforts at inclusion. Critics see DEI as nothing more than a woke agenda in the workplace. Though DEI training has faced pushback, implementing DEI programs has many benefits, including increased profits and lower turnover rates. It also adds broader perspectives within the company, which can help a business grow by reaching new customers and contacts. Not everyone likes focusing so much on DEI in the workplace, though. Critics believe it puts a person's diversity ahead of his or her skills and experience. They also believe many of the acts of DEI training are performative and lack signs of any measurable change in the workplace.

Having a diverse workplace may bring new perspectives to projects. Diversity includes having people of different genders, ages, ethnicities, and sexual orientations.

CHAPTER THREE

"Where Woke Goes to Die"

Along with his wife and three young children, Florida governor Ron DeSantis walked onstage at the Tampa Convention Center on November 8, 2022. He had just won a decisive victory for a second term as the state's governor. His victory speech was not just about an election win, however. It was about triumphing over one of DeSantis's biggest foes: the woke ideology sweeping the nation.

DeSantis thanked his supporters. Then he painted a grim picture of parts of the United States where he believed being woke had influenced the government. He cited an increase in crime, higher taxes, and a loss of American principles in these areas. "The woke agenda has caused millions of Americans to leave these jurisdictions for greener pastures. Now this great exodus of Americans—for those folks . . . Florida has served as the promised land," said DeSantis.[23]

The reason they chose Florida, according to DeSantis, was because of the way its citizens and government have shielded the state from wokeness. DeSantis praised Florida for maintaining traditional values that he believes have been eliminated by woke governments elsewhere. "We have embraced freedom. We have maintained law and order. We have protected the rights of parents. We have respected our taxpayers. And we reject woke ideology," said DeSantis. "We fight the woke in the legislature. We fight the woke in the schools. We fight the woke in the corporations. We will never,

Ron DeSantis was in the US House of Representatives from 2013 to 2018. He became Florida's governor in 2019.

> "We fight the woke in the legislature. We fight the woke in the schools. We fight the woke in the corporations. We will never, ever surrender to the woke mob. Florida is where woke goes to die."
> —Ron DeSantis, governor of Florida

ever surrender to the woke mob. Florida is where woke goes to die."[24]

For conservatives like DeSantis, the word *woke* represents an overcorrection in social policies. Conservatives and liberals alike agree that social injustices, such as racism and sexism, must be addressed. Yet conservatives argue that the woke agenda goes too far in its efforts to address the problems. One of the most cited examples of this is affirmative action. This is a government policy that creates opportunities for people who have traditionally been marginalized. The goal is to level the playing field for people who have faced discrimination. Some conservatives, however, believe it has created a situation where marginalized groups receive special treatment at the expense of the majority. This type of perceived overcorrection is commonly referred to as reverse discrimination.

Beyond that, conservatives say the woke agenda represents a liberal overthrow of traditional values. They also say it restricts individual freedoms. A dispute between then-President Donald Trump and Twitter provides an example of this belief. In January 2021, Trump was upset that he lost the presidential election. He made a speech to his supporters, who then stormed the US Capitol. Days later, Twitter permanently banned Trump's account. It said tweets Trump had made incited violence at the Capitol, which violated Twitter's terms of service. Trump issued a statement saying his right to free speech had been violated by the ban. Late in 2022, Twitter allowed Trump to return. However, that did not change the conservative belief that corporations with a woke agenda are infringing on free speech.

Another conservative criticism of the woke agenda is that being woke is nothing more than performative activism. This type of activism—which is also known as slacktivism, clicktivism, and performative wokeness—often appears inauthentic. People may post something on social media to make it appear as though they support a cause, for example. While their post may look good, the person is not actually doing anything to aid the cause, such as calling lawmakers, raising money, or volunteering. The surge in the popularity of wokeism is often considered by critics to be superficial at best.

The Anti-Woke Agenda

In response to the rise of wokeism, conservatives created an anti-woke agenda. In broad terms, the anti-woke agenda seeks to conserve the nation's existing social order. Many conservatives value tradition and continuity from the past to the present. They believe the government should not interfere in the lives of its citizens. The anti-woke agenda lines up with traditional conservative values that are relevant to issues such as policing, gender identity, and education.

After George Floyd's death, many woke protesters demanded that police forces be defunded. They sought to end police brutality, which affects Black people disproportionately. In 2021, for example, Black people represented 13 percent of the nation's population and 27 percent of all fatal police shootings. Woke protesters also noted the racist origins of the police forces in the country, which began as patrols that captured escaped enslaved people and returned them to their enslavers. Defunding the police became a rallying cry among protesters. Defunding plans differed,

In 2020, Pew Research conducted a poll to see how Americans felt about funding the police. Seventy-three percent of people said they either wanted spending to stay the same or to increase.

but in general they sought to reduce the number of officers on the streets. In their place, social workers, mental health experts, drug counselors, and other professionals would serve community needs.

The anti-woke agenda, on the other hand, calls for strong law enforcement. Police officers are viewed as vital leaders who create and maintain social order, safety, and peace within their communities by ensuring laws are followed. Many conservative lawmakers stand closely aligned with law enforcement agencies. "Republicans are proud to support the police, to stand with the men and women in blue while Democrats are demonizing and vilifying the brave men and women in law enforcement," said Senator Ted Cruz in 2021.[25] As a sign of this support, conservative rallies often feature a black and white American flag with a thin blue line on it. The thin blue line represents the police as the barrier between good and bad, chaos and order in US society. The flag began appearing around 2014, which was when a group called Blue Lives Matter formed. The flag was used to advocate for police officers in the wake of the police killings of several Black men, including Michael Brown. Critics find the flag disrespectful, and it has been banned in some places.

Another issue of disagreement between the woke and anti-woke agendas centers on the LGBTQ+ community. A 2020 survey by the Center for American Progress revealed that more than one in three LGBTQ+ Americans had faced discrimination in the past year. LGBTQ+ youth are also more likely to experience homelessness and suicide than their straight peers. The woke agenda generally supports members of this community. This includes fighting for issues such as legally protecting same-sex marriages, teaching sex education that is inclusive of LGBTQ+ experiences, and affirming a person's gender.

The anti-woke agenda generally works to stop laws and practices that affirm LGBTQ+ people. Between 2020 and 2023, more than one hundred bills were introduced in state legislatures that targeted transgender people. These laws sought to restrict transgender medical care for youth, stop transgender people from using bathrooms and locker rooms that match their gender, and prevent transgender students from participating in non-coed sports.

Though these bills are numerous, perhaps none has received more attention than Florida's Parental Rights Bill, nicknamed the "Don't Say Gay Bill." Governor DeSantis signed it into law in March 2022. It stops teachers from discussing gender identity or sexuality in kindergarten through third grade. Supporters believe it transfers power from schools to parents regarding sexuality

Wokeness as a Religion

The percentage of people who belong to religious communities has dropped significantly in the United States. A 2021 Gallup poll showed only 47 percent of Americans belonged to a church, synagogue, or mosque. That was much lower than the first time the poll was taken in 1937, when the number stood at 73 percent. Some anti-woke critics say wokeness has replaced religion, suggesting that it provides followers the same sense of purpose and belonging as religion once did.

"The demise of religion among American youth is greatly exaggerated," conservative journalist David French wrote sarcastically. "It turns out that America isn't raising a new generation of unbelievers. Instead, rising in the heart of deep-blue America are the zealots of a new religious faith. They're the intersectionals, they're fully woke, and the heretics don't stand a chance." French also compared the tenets of the Christian faith with wokeness:

> There's an animating purpose—fighting injustice, racism, and inequality. There's the original sin of 'privilege.' There's a conversion experience—becoming 'woke.' And much as the Christian church puts a premium on each person's finding his or her precise role in the body of Christ, intersectionality can provide a person with a specific purpose and role based on individual identity and experience.

David French, "Intersectionality, the Dangerous Faith," *National Review, March 6, 2018. www.nationalreview.com.*

issues, allowing parents to introduce these concepts when they feel their child is ready.

"We will make sure that parents can send their kids to school to get an education, not an indoctrination," DeSantis said after signing the bill. "Elementary school kids should not have woke gender ideology injected into the curriculum. That is inappropriate, that's not what we want in our school system," he added.[26] Marco Rubio, a US senator representing Florida, also defended the bill. "We send our kids to school to learn how to read, to learn how to write, to learn about history, to acquire academic proficiency," Rubio said. "We don't send kids to school so the schools can raise our kids, we send them so they can teach them. Raising kids is the job of parents and families, not schools."[27]

Critics disagreed, saying the new law was discriminatory and vague. For instance, the law notes that schools are required to notify parents if their child seeks health care, offering parents the option to decline the services. But it wasn't clear what "health care" meant in this context. The law concerned many people. The Trevor Project, a nonprofit organization working to prevent suicide among LGBTQ+ youth, explained why this portion of the bill was especially troublesome. A teacher or other school professional may be forced to "out" an LGBTQ+ student to their parents or guardians. If the teacher keeps the student's confidence, he or she would be breaking the law. Outing a student with unsupportive caretakers has the potential of leading to violence, homelessness, and even suicide.

Critical Race Theory

One of the biggest rallying points around the anti-woke agenda is Critical Race Theory (CRT). For decades, CRT was a topic in high-level academia but was rarely discussed by the general public. Then, during national discussions about race after George Floyd's death in 2020, *CRT* became a buzzword almost overnight. It appeared in news broadcasts, political debates, and even social media memes. Everyone seemed to have an opinion about this once obscure theory.

CRT is the study of how race impacts US society and its laws. The framework of CRT arose just after the civil rights movement of the 1960s. The Civil Rights Act of 1964 had legally ended discrimination based on race, color, religion, sex, and national origin. The deep causes of racism remained unaddressed, however. Historically, people held the mistaken belief that one race was superior to another. The belief did not disappear when the Civil Rights Act became law. This created a situation where overt racism, such as segregation, was prohibited by law, but

Christopher Rufo

On his website, Christopher Rufo describes himself as a writer, filmmaker, and activist. He is also the person who helped draw the mainstream media's attention to CRT. While doing research, Rufo discovered information about anti-bias training occurring in Seattle, Washington. He wrote about what he had uncovered in an article for the *City-Journal* magazine.

In the article, Rufo said that the city "sent an email inviting 'white City employees' to attend a training session on 'Interrupting Internalized Racial Superiority and Whiteness,' a program designed to help white workers examine their 'complicity in the system of white supremacy' and 'interrupt racism in ways that are accountable to Black, Indigenous and People of Color.'"[1]

Rufo continued with his research, ultimately discovering academic writings about CRT. In September 2020, Rufo appeared on Fox News. He introduced the viewers to the term *critical race theory*. Then he said, "Conservatives need to wake up. This is an existential threat to the United States. And the bureaucracy, even under Trump, is being weaponized against core American values."[2] Rufo's admonition pushed CRT into the spotlight and created a new buzzword in the culture wars.

[1] *Christopher F. Rufo, "Cult Programming in Seattle,"* City-Journal, *July 8, 2020. www.city-journal.org.*
[2] *Benjamin Wallace-Wells, "How a Conservative Activist Invented the Conflict over Critical Race Theory,"* New Yorker, *June 18, 2021. www.newyorker.com.*

subtler forms of discrimination remained.

Because of its quick rise in the mainstream, CRT left many people confused about what it truly meant. "Critical race theory is practiced by any number of people and groups who recognize that colorblindness is an aspiration, but it's not the reality in American society," said Kimberlé Crenshaw, one of founders of CRT. "And to survive and to thrive, you have to be aware of how race plays a role. You have to pass it on to your children. You have to practice it in your workplace. You practice it in the stores. You practice it wherever you go."[28]

The lens of CRT provides people with a way to see the impacts of the nation's laws on discrimination. Statistics show, for example, that people of color are more likely to be denied loans, be suspected of a crime, and be victims of police brutality than their white peers. This phenomenon is often referred to as white privilege. Ibram X. Kendi, an anti-racist activist and professor, explained it this way: "White privileges are the relative advantages racism affords to people identified as white, whether white people recognize them or deny them."[29]

Not everyone agrees with viewing society through the lens of CRT. Critics suggest that it is too narrowly focused on race as the driving force behind power dynamics in the nation. They dislike how it divides society into either oppressors or victims, which gives little room for personal responsibility. In this view, white people are the oppressors and people of color are the victims.

> "Critical race theory is practiced by any number of people and groups who recognize that colorblindness is an aspiration, but it's not the reality in American society. And to survive and to thrive, you have to be aware of how race plays a role. You have to pass it on to your children. You have to practice it in your workplace. You practice it in the stores. You practice it wherever you go."
> —Kimberlé Crenshaw, civil rights activist and legal scholar

Donald Trump was president from 2017 to 2021. Many of his supporters liked his outspoken behavior.

Critics believe CRT supporters want to dismantle the systems that the United States is founded upon because CRT supporters see those systems as inherently racist.

The backlash against CRT appeared almost as soon as the term appeared in the mainstream media. It quickly morphed from an academic theory into a political weapon. CRT opposition ramped up in July 2020, when a graphic appeared on the website for the Smithsonian's National Museum of African American History and Culture, listing several values of the nation's culture that have been dominated by white people. These values included the nuclear family unit, Christianity, the concept that hard work leads to success, and a national history told from the experiences of European immigrants.

Days later, President Trump called out the divisiveness of this graphic while speaking about CRT at the White House History Conference. "This document alleged that concepts such as hard work, rational thinking, the nuclear family, and belief in God were not values that unite all Americans, but were instead aspects of 'whiteness,'" said Trump. "This is offensive and outrageous to Americans of every ethnicity, and it is especially harmful to children of minority backgrounds who should be uplifted, not disparaged."[30]

While the graphic was later removed from the museum's website, Trump continued to speak out against CRT for the remainder of his time in office. His comments largely echoed the thoughts of many of his supporters across the nation. In September 2020, Trump made his strongest stand against CRT when he issued an executive order to all federal agencies. It asked them to stop any government diversity trainings that taught about CRT or white privilege, which he called "divisive, anti-American propaganda."[31]

Some parents worry that teachers try to indoctrinate students with beliefs that the parents don't approve of. CRT is one topic some parents don't want discussed in schools.

Banning Woke in Schools

Though President Joe Biden repealed Trump's executive order when he took office in January 2021, the debate surrounding CRT continued. No place was the debate more heated than in America's schools. At stake was whether to use CRT-influenced curriculums in classrooms. After Floyd's death, many schools addressed the racial issues going on in society. In some districts, this meant a more intentional study of the nation's racial inequalities and the events connected to them. Experts said CRT is not taught in K–12 classrooms because it is too advanced for these grades. Some parents worried the idea behind CRT still had a large influence on school curriculums, even if the theory itself was not taught.

Parents and lawmakers in several states protested CRT curriculum changes within America's classrooms. They saw teaching CRT as a wedge that divided people by race. They feared it would increase tensions between white people and people of color, splitting society apart and ultimately weakening the nation. They also disliked the idea that the systems of the nation are inherently racist, suggesting instead these systems have failed to live up to their ideals of liberty and equality. Some critics also believe CRT unfairly blames white people today for racial injustices of the past, creating a sense of guilt in white students for actions they have not personally committed.

At a 2021 school board meeting in Tennessee, a mother said that her seven-year-old daughter had come home upset. The girl had told her mother, "I'm ashamed that I'm white. Is there something wrong with me? Why am I hated so much?"[32] The board denied that CRT was part of the curriculum, though parents believed the values aligned with CRT had slipped into the schools nonetheless. The father of an elementary school boy also spoke up, recounting the boy's experience with an online lesson about Dr. Martin Luther King Jr. "It started out very beautifully talking about Dr. King and his speech and children from different backgrounds all coming together," the father said. "But then it started talking about the deep and dark portions of what happened during the 1960s." He went to say that his son "was ashamed to be an American after reading this lesson. He didn't want to be American. He saw all of the evil that had been attributed [to Americans] over the years."[33]

School board meetings across the nation became battlegrounds of CRT. Between January 2021 and September 2022, lawmakers in forty-four states introduced bills that would either ban CRT in the classroom or restrict how teachers discuss race. Texas was one of the states that passed such bills into law. Dan Patrick, lieutenant governor of Texas, said:

> Texans reject critical race theory and other so-called 'woke' philosophies that maintain that one race or sex is inherently superior to another race or sex or that any individual, by virtue of his or her race or sex, is inherently racist, sexist, or oppressive. These divisive concepts have been inserted into curriculums around the state, but they have no place in Texas schools.[34]

Some parents have protested teaching CRT in classrooms. Many Republican-led states have introduced legislation to address how racism and race are discussed at schools.

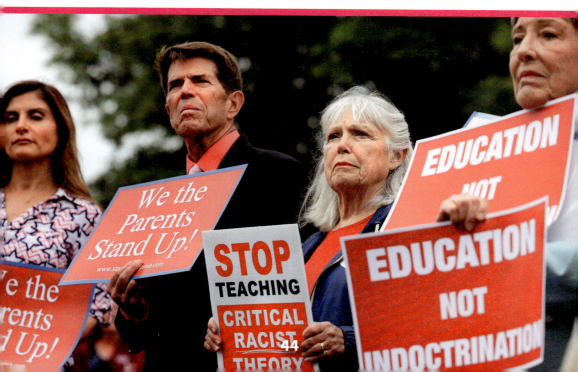

In April 2022, a Florida law signed by Governor DeSantis received national attention for its wide-ranging effort to stop CRT. The Stop Wrongs Against Our Kids and Employees Act—called Stop WOKE for short—did not mention CRT by name, though it addressed many issues closely connected to the theory. The law prohibited teachers from telling students that a person could be privileged or oppressed based on skin color. The law also limited what teachers could say about race in classrooms and what employers could teach about race in company trainings. Violating the law could result in termination or loss of school funding. "We believe an important component of freedom in the state of Florida is the freedom from having oppressive ideologies imposed upon you without your consent, whether it be in the classroom or in the workplace. And we decided to do something about it," DeSantis said.[35]

Florida's new law had barely been passed when people began to challenge it in the court system. People opposed to the law worried it was an attempt to erase parts of US history that made some white people uncomfortable. They were also concerned it would have a negative effect on how openly people could talk about race. Equality Florida, the state's largest civil rights group, issued a statement regarding the Stop WOKE law. It said, "The so-called Stop WOKE Act would censor honest conversations about Black history, LGBTQ history, and the root causes of injustice and discrimination in schools and workplaces."[36]

> "Texans reject critical race theory and other so-called 'woke' philosophies that maintain that one race or sex is inherently superior to another race or sex or that any individual, by virtue of his or her race or sex, is inherently racist, sexist, or oppressive. These divisive concepts have been inserted into curriculums around the state, but they have no place in Texas schools."
> —Dan Patrick, lieutenant governor of Texas

CHAPTER FOUR

Life in a Woke Nation

Shortly after taking office in January 2021, President Joe Biden began nominating candidates to leadership positions within federal agencies. These nominees generally don't make news headlines—they are regular people going about their jobs like millions of other Americans. That was not the case, however, for Biden's nominee to the Office of Assistant Secretary for Health. For this position, Biden had nominated a transgender doctor named Rachel Levine. Her gender identity drew national headlines. When members of the Senate confirmed Levine in March, she became the highest-ranking openly transgender person in the federal government.

Levine's historic confirmation generated controversy. It happened during a national debate about medical care accessibility for transgender people. Many conservatives believed Biden was pushing a woke agenda with Levine's nomination, and they found his choice troubling. Travis Webber is a vice president at the conservative group Family Research Council. He condemned the nomination, saying, "Levine may be the most extreme radical ever confirmed by the Senate."[37] In contrast, many members of the LGBTQ+ community saw Biden's choice of Levine as a step in the right direction. "With the confirmation of Dr. Rachel Levine, we are one step closer to a government that mirrors the beautiful diversity of its people," said Alphonso David, president of the Human Rights Campaign.[38]

Before becoming the US assistant secretary for health, Rachel Levine worked as a doctor and professor. She was also the secretary of health for Pennsylvania.

In March 2022, a year after taking office, Levine was named one of *USA Today*'s "Women of the Year." It's an honor the newspaper gives to women who have made a lasting impact on the nation. Much like Levine's confirmation, the award drew the ire of many Americans. Charlie Kirk, founder of the conservative group Turning Point USA, went to Twitter after hearing Levine had received the award. "Richard Levine spent 54 years of his life as a man. He had a wife and family. He 'transitioned' to being a woman in 2011, Joe Biden appointed Levine to be a 4-Star Admiral, and now *USA Today* has named 'Rachel' Levine as a 'Woman of the Year.' Where are the feminists?"[39] Kirk's post referred to Levine by the wrong gender, a practice known as misgendering. Kirk had also called Levine by her birth name, a disrespectful practice known as deadnaming. Twitter suspended Kirk for his comments.

Kirk wasn't the only one in hot water over his thoughts on Levine. The Babylon Bee, a website that produces satirical news stories from a conservative perspective, wrote a piece

Tweets can be up to 280 characters long. In 2022, more than 368 million people used Twitter.

with the headline "The Babylon Bee's Man of The Year is Rachel Levine" and posted it on Twitter. Like Kirk, the Babylon Bee was suspended from Twitter because of hateful conduct. If the site promised to take down the post, Twitter would restore its access. Seth Dillion, CEO of the Babylon Bee, refused the offer. "We're not deleting anything. Truth is not hate speech. If the cost of telling the truth is the loss of our Twitter account, then so be it," Dillon wrote.[40]

The conversation surrounding Levine was another battle in the nation's culture wars. Addressing wokeness and the tug-of-war between the

> "We're not deleting anything. Truth is not hate speech. If the cost of telling the truth is the loss of our Twitter account, then so be it."
> —Seth Dillion, CEO of the Babylon Bee after its Twitter account was suspended

viewpoints became a part of everyday life, splitting Americans deeply. Divisions appeared not just in politics and on social media platforms, but also in classrooms, sports arenas, public libraries, movies, and even Disney World. Nothing in US culture appeared immune from wokeness and the pushback that came with it. It became a leading element in shaping the nation. Along with it came a byproduct: cancel culture.

Cancel Culture

Some people fear being canceled. At its most basic level, canceling means calling out people and withdrawing support from them. It removes their power within the culture at large. This typically happens when a person says or does something that could be

Political Correctness

Political correctness is the forerunner to cancel culture. It avoids language that offends people. Political correctness is based upon a linguistics theory called the Sapir-Whorf Hypothesis. It says that a person's perception of reality is shaped by their thoughts, and their thoughts are shaped by the language they use. Using racist language, for example, would result in racist thoughts, which would create a racist perception of reality. In theory, using language that is politically correct would help to root out these problems.

Political correctness began in the 1970s and grew slowly until it peaked in the 1990s. Much like cancel culture, some argued that it limited their speech. "We find free speech under assault throughout the United States," said President George H. W. Bush in 1991. "The notion of political correctness has ignited controversy across the land." Nearly thirty years later, President Trump said similar things about cancel culture. "The goal of cancel culture is to make decent Americans live in fear of being fired, expelled, shamed, humiliated and driven from society as we know it," Trump said in 2020.

Ari Shapiro, et al, "How Cancel Culture Became Politicized—Just Like Political Correctness," NPR, July 26, 2021. www.nrp.org.

offensive, such as making a racist comment or committing sexual harassment.

The concept of cancel culture is not new. Banishing people for violating social norms has existed in many cultures for thousands of years. What is new, however, is the way Americans have weaponized its power. Slang use of the word *cancel* originated in Black communities, according to University of Virginia media studies professor Meredith Clark.

Much like the word *woke*, the meaning of *cancel culture* has shifted, expanded, and morphed over time depending on who used it and why. Cancel culture grew out of the civil rights era of the 1960s. Protesters commonly boycotted businesses that allowed segregation during this time. Cancel culture was a natural outgrowth of those boycotts. Much like the boycotts, cancel culture allowed marginalized groups to push back against people who violated the group's values, beliefs, or rights. Canceling served as a method for keeping powerful public figures accountable for their actions. As social media grew, it amplified

Can't Be Canceled

Some Americans have argued that no one can truly be canceled, no matter what people say about them on social media or elsewhere. Some canceled celebrities, politicians, and business leaders have made successful comebacks. In 2021, for example, Dr. Seuss Enterprises decided to no longer publish six of the author's titles because they included racist content. People loudly criticized the decision, claiming Dr. Seuss had been canceled. Few people were ready to give up on the world's best-selling children's author. Within days of the decision, nine of the ten books on the Amazon bestseller list belonged to Dr. Seuss. Some librarians, too, worked to keep the canceled books on the shelves, including context notes with the books that could help start discussions about what topics might be problematic. And in 2022, Netflix announced it would produce five new animated specials and series based on the author's work.

these marginalized voices. Mainstream media picked up on this trend, and cancel culture began to spread and take on new power.

As cancel culture grew in influence, it morphed and was no longer restricted to marginalized groups and people in positions of power. Instead, anyone was fair game to be canceled. The range of people who were canceled—and the reasons for being canceled—were numerous. Model and actress Chrissy Teigen was canceled for cyberbullying. *Harry Potter* author J. K. Rowling was canceled over comments that were seen as anti-transgender. Comedian Dave Chapelle found himself canceled when his Netflix special included transphobic jokes. New York governor Andrew Cuomo was canceled and later had to resign after sexual harassment allegations. Comedian Ellen DeGeneres was canceled after being accused of creating a toxic work environment.

> "Unfortunately, too many on the left, wielding the cudgel of 'cancel culture,' have decided that certain forms of censorship and speech and idea suppression are positive things that will advance social justice."
> — Dan Kovalik, author of *Cancel This Book*

The uptick in people being canceled did not sit well with some Americans. Critics believed canceling people was a form of censorship. They argued that people could not speak or act freely for fear of potentially facing personal or professional ruin by being canceled. For critics, cancel culture was not a way to keep people accountable. It was a way to punish people who speak their minds. Dan Kovalik, author of *Cancel This Book*, explained it this way: "Unfortunately, too many on the left, wielding the cudgel of 'cancel culture,' have decided that certain forms of censorship and speech and idea suppression are positive things that will advance social justice."[41]

It wasn't just conservatives who felt cancel culture had gone too far. Some liberals also believed the practice was no longer useful and was limiting open discourse. James Carville, a

Punishment or Accountability?

In 2022, Pew Research conducted a survey. It wanted to see whether US adults thought calling someone out on social media for potentially offensive content was a good or bad thing, and how that broke down between Democrats and Republicans.

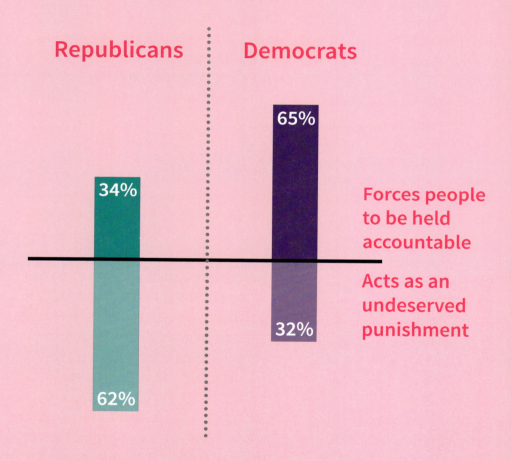

Numbers do not equal 100 percent because people who didn't answer the question aren't shown.

Source: Emily A. Vogels, "A Growing Share of Americans Are Familiar with 'Cancel Culture,'" *Pew Research*, June 9, 2022. www.pewresearch.org.

Democratic pundit and campaign strategist for former president Bill Clinton, expanded on this idea in a 2021 interview for *Vox*. He said, "Wokeness is a problem, and everyone knows it. It's hard to talk to anybody today—and I talk to lots of people in the Democratic Party—who doesn't say this. But they don't want to say it out loud." When asked why they wouldn't say it out loud, he said it was "because they'll get clobbered or canceled."[42]

Corporate Wokeness

As woke culture spread across the country, it also trickled into corporate America. In 2015, *New York Times* columnist Ross Douthat created the term *woke capital* for a new trend he was seeing. The term described how businesses were tapping into hot-button social issues not only to earn a profit but also to have cultural relevance. In the years since Douthat first noticed the trend, the use of woke capital has become widespread.

Attorney Ashley Keller condemned woke companies at a November 2021 meeting of the Federalist Society, a powerful conservative legal organization. The list of woke corporations Keller called out included Facebook, Google, Amazon, Coca-Cola, Twitter, and Walmart. He claimed that they had become part of

Good for Business?

Many people accuse woke companies of virtue signaling, which is the practice of expressing opinions to appear socially conscious or morally correct. Critics also believe this is largely performative, and the companies don't make meaningful changes to match the images they are projecting.

Younger consumers are, on average, more liberal than older consumers. Younger consumers are also the ones with the largest influence on the market. To tap into this group's spending potential, advertisers focus on what drives these consumers and align marketing campaigns with their values. Many of these younger consumers care about issues that are part of the woke agenda. This has led some business leaders to believe that being woke is simply good for business.

"the swelling ranks of so-called 'woke' people, who are completely and unabashedly opposed to individual rights."[43] To push back, between 2021 and 2022, forty-four bills were introduced in seventeen conservative states to penalize corporations for siding with the woke agenda. The laws would prevent corporations from participating in certain markets and industries if they have taken a woke stance on fossil fuels, firearms, gay marriage, or any other social issue.

In one instance from January 2022, the state treasurer for West Virginia, Riley Moore, cut the state's investment ties with BlackRock. BlackRock is the world's largest money manager, with more than $10 trillion in assets under management. The company expressed interest in environmental causes, such as decarbonization. This is the process of reducing greenhouse gas emissions from burning fossil fuels such as coal and natural gas. West Virginia is the nation's second-largest coal producer and its fifth-largest natural gas producer. "They're using the power of their capital to push their ideas and ideology down onto the rest of us," said Moore.[44]

Moore's decision to end investments with BlackRock was the first time any state had stopped doing business with a firm because of its stance on Environmental, Social, and Governance (ESG) impacts. ESG is a screening method some businesses use to determine whether they should invest in a company or industry. A firm using an ESG would consider how an investment impacts the natural world, people and social causes, and the firm's operation. These considerations are separate from the financial soundness of an investment and are often thought of as a woke viewpoint on investing.

When companies that use ESG decide not to invest in a certain industry, it can cause financial losses for that industry. Many states tried to stop this from happening. For example, Moore pushed for a new bill in West Virginia's state legislature, which became law in March 2022. It penalized banks that took a stance against fossil fuels by refusing to offer contracts to them from the state of West Virginia. Moore also formed a fifteen-state coalition

At first, Disney was silent when the "Don't Say Gay Bill" was proposed. When employees at Disney voiced their displeasure, Disney leaders finally spoke out.

to push back on companies that take stances against the coal, oil, and natural gas industries.

Just a month after Moore's law passed, a woke corporate dispute began in Florida. It was between Governor Ron DeSantis and one of the state's largest companies: Disney. When the "Don't Say Gay Bill" went to the legislature, employees at Disney were outraged that the company had not taken a strong stance against the bill, forcing CEO Bob Chapek into an awkward position. He ultimately contacted DeSantis. Speaking on behalf of Disney, Chapek communicated the company's concerns that the "Don't Say Gay Bill" had the potential to discriminate against people in the LGBTQ+ community.

DeSantis ultimately struck back by stripping Walt Disney World of a special legal status it had held since 1967. The state allowed Disney to govern an area of nearly 40 square miles (104 sq km) in a manner much like a city does. Disney collected its own taxes and provided its own infrastructure such as water, electricity, and emergency services. The goal was to give Disney independence without burdening the local taxpayers as the corporation grew. Many unknowns remained about how the change in status would affect Disney, the state of Florida, and local taxpayers over the long run. It appeared likely, however, that it would make business more difficult for Disney. The company would need to go through standard government processes to do its business. For example, a new building project would require approval by the local government. In the past, the special status would have allowed Disney to bypass this step.

The Future of Woke

Wokeism and the push against it ramped up in the 2020s. Woke culture didn't spring up out of nowhere, however. Some Americans had spoken about it for years or even decades. For most of that time, the idea was not visible in mainstream white America. Then everything seemed to change almost at once. The death of George Floyd and the racial reckoning that came afterward made wokeness dramatically more visible.

The woke agenda and the anti-woke agenda are likely to remain prominent in American culture. While the word *woke* itself may fall out of favor, the push and pull between liberal and conservative viewpoints will persist. It's a struggle that has been part of the nation since its beginning. Yet in many ways, the woke ideology is unique to the modern era. Its roots developed in the nation's Black communities at a time when overt discrimination, segregation, and violence were prevalent. Eventually, it spread across social media, moving in ways that were so fast and so far-reaching that they would have been nearly impossible to imagine just a few decades ago. Whether being woke is good or bad for the country and its people lies in the perspective of each individual.

Conversations about being woke can become intense. But people can try to understand others' perspectives by listening respectfully to them.

SOURCE NOTES

Introduction: Making History or Defiling It?

1. Quoted in "Lizzo Played James Madison's Crystal Flute," *NPR*, September 28, 2022. www.npr.org.

2. Quoted in Candace Owens Podcast, "Cardi B and Lizzo Are Puppets," *YouTube*, September 29, 2022. www.youtube.com.

3. Matt Walsh, "Lizzo Playing James Madison's Flute Was a Form of Racial Retribution," *Twitter*, September 28, 2022. https://twitter.com.

Chapter One: The Origins of Woke

4. Quoted in "Obama on Call-Out Culture," *New York Times*, August 10, 2020. www.nytimes.com.

5. Quoted in Rueb and Taylor, "Obama on Call-Out Culture."

6. Quoted in Aja Romero, "Stay Woke," *Vox*, October 9, 2020. www.vox.com.

7. Quoted in Romero, "Stay Woke."

8. Quoted in "Why We Say Woke," *Brut*, n.d. www.brut.media.

9. Malcolm X, "The Ballot or the Bullet," *Social Justice Speeches*, April 3, 1964. www.edchange.org.

10. Quoted in Ishena Robinson, "How Woke Went from 'Black' to 'Bad,'" *Legal Defense Fund*, August 26, 2022. www.naacpldf.org.

11. Quoted in Jonah E. Bromwich, "Erykah Badu's Complicated Relationship with 'Wokeness,'" *Vulture*, January 31, 2018. www.vulture.com.

12. Quoted in "What Does 'Woke' Actually Mean?" *KPBS*, March 11, 2022. www.kpbs.org.

13. Quoted in Reggie Ugwu, "Erykah Badu Helped Define 'Wokeness,'" *New York Times*, February 6, 2019. www.nytimes.com.

14. Peggy Noonan, "Democrats Need to Face Down the Woke," *Wall Street Journal*, November 11, 2021. www.wsj.com

Chapter Two: Being Woke

15. Quoted in "Timeline of Events Since George Floyd's Arrest and Murder," *AP News*, January 20, 2022. https://apnews.com.

16. Quoted in Khaleda Rahman, "George Floyd's Brother Urges Americans to 'Stay Woke,'" *Newsweek*, May 24, 2021. www.newsweek.com.

17. Quoted in "The 1619 Project," *PBS News Weekend*, August 18, 2019. www.pbs.org.

18. Quoted in Hannah Grossman, "Why Schools Adopted the 1619 Project," *Fox News*, April 11, 2022. www.foxnews.com.

19. Quoted in Mike Gonzalez, "1619 and the Poisoned Well of Identity Politics," *Heritage Foundation*, November 19, 2020. www.heritage.org.

20. Quoted in "Kimberlé Crenshaw on Intersectionality," *Columbia Law School*, June 8, 2017. www.law.columbia.edu.

21. Quoted in Katy Steinmetz, "She Coined the Term 'Intersectionality' over 30 Years Ago. Here's What It Means to Her Today," *Time*, February 20, 2020. https://time.com.

22. Quoted in "Inside the Mind of Ben Shapiro," *Economist*, March 28, 2019. www.economist.com.

Chapter Three: "Where Woke Goes to Die"

23. Quoted in "Ron DeSantis 2022 Florida Governor Race Victory Speech," *YouTube*, November 8, 2022. www.youtube.com.

24. Quoted in "Ron DeSantis 2022 Florida Governor Race Victory Speech."

25. Ted Cruz, "Dems Have Called to Defund the Police," *YouTube*, July 22, 2021. www.youtube.com.

26. Quoted in "Gov. Ron DeSantis Addresses 'Woke Gender Ideology' Ahead of 'Don't Say Gay' Law Taking Effect," *CBS Miami*, June 15, 2022. www.cbsnews.com.

27. Quoted in "Rubio Defends 'Don't Say Gay' Bill," *Hill*, March 16, 2022. https://thehill.com.

28. Quoted in "Ideas That Make Up Critical Race Theory Have Been Around Long Before It Got Its Name," *NPR*, September 13, 2022. www.npr.org.

29. Ibram X. Kendi, "The Greatest White Privilege Is Life Itself," *Atlantic*, October 24, 2019. www.theatlantic.com.

30. Donald Trump, "President Trump Remarks at White House History Conference," *C-SPAN*, September 17, 2020. www.c-span.org.

31. Quoted in Matthew S. Schwartz, "Trump Tells Agencies to End Trainings on 'White Privilege' and 'Critical Race Theory,'" *NPR*, September 5, 2020. www.npr.org.

32. Quoted in Chris Butler, "Williamson County Parents Warn Critical Race Theory Has Already Entered Their Public School System," *Tennessee Star*, April 21, 2021. https://tennesseestar.com.

33. Quoted in Butler, "Williamson County Parents."

34. Dan Patrick, "Statement on the Passage of Senate Bill 2202," *Office of the Lieutenant Governor*, April 28, 2021. www.ltgov.texas.gov.

35. Quoted in John Kennedy, "DeSantis Signs into Law 'Stop WOKE Act' to Restrict Race Discussions in Florida," *Tallahassee Democrat*, April 22, 2022. www.tallahassee.com.

36. Quoted in "Oppose HB 7/SB 148," *Equality Florida*, n.d. www.aclufl.org.

Chapter Four: Life in a Woke Nation

37. Quoted in David Crary, "A First: US Senate Confirms Transgender Doctor for Key Post," *AP News*, March 24, 2021. https://apnews.com.

38. Quoted in Dan Diamond et al., "Historic Transgender Nominee, Confirmed as Assistant Health Secretary," *Washington Post*, March 24, 2021. www.washingtonpost.com.

39. Charlie Kirk, "USA Today Names Actual Man as One of Its 'Women of the Year,'" *Charlie Kirk Show*, March 15, 2022. https://thecharliekirkshow.com.

40. Quoted in Gerrard Kaonga, "Why Was the Babylon Bee Suspended by Twitter? CEO Seth Dillon Reacts to Ban," *Newsweek*, March 21, 2022. www.newsweek.com.

41. Quoted in Aja Romano, "The Second Wave of 'Cancel Culture,'" *Vox*, May 5, 2021. www.vox.com.

42. Quoted in Sean Illing, "'Wokeness Is a Problem,'" *Vox*, April 27, 2021. www.vox.com.

43. Quoted in Ian Millhiser, "The Federalist Society's Newest Enemy: Corporate America," *Vox*, November 18, 2021. www.vox.com.

44. Pete Schroeder, "How Republican-Led States Are Targeting Wall Street with 'Anti-Woke' Laws," *Reuters*, July 6, 2022. www.reuters.com.

FOR FURTHER RESEARCH

Books

John Allen, *Cancel Culture: Social Justice or Mob Rule?* San Diego, CA: ReferencePoint Press, 2022.

Kate Conley, *Social Media and Modern Society*. Minneapolis, MN: Abdo, 2022.

Sue Bradford Edwards, *Cancel Culture*. Minneapolis, MN: Abdo, 2022.

Internet Sources

Perry Bacon Jr., "Why Attacking 'Cancel Culture' and 'Woke' People Is Becoming the GOP's New Political Strategy," *FiveThirtyEight*, March 17, 2021. https://fivethirtyeight.com.

Aja Romano, "A History of 'Wokeness,'" *Vox*, October 9, 2020. www.vox.com.

Michael Ruiz, "What Does 'Woke' Mean?" *Fox News*, December 7, 2021. www.foxnews.com.

Related Organizations

American Civil Liberties Union (ACLU)
www.aclu.org
The ACLU is an organization that began in 1920 to protect and preserve people's civil rights. It works through courts, communities, and legislative bodies.

The Heritage Foundation
www.heritage.org
The Heritage Foundation is a conservative think tank based in Washington, DC. Its goal is to encourage policies that further individual freedoms, limit government interference, strengthen national defense, and protect traditional values in the United States.

National Center for Transgender Equality
https://transequality.org
The National Center for Transgender Equality is an organization dedicated to changing policies to create a greater awareness and understanding of transgender people.

INDEX

activism, 8–9, 16, 26–27, 34, 39–40
American Historical Association, 25
anti-woke agenda, 34, 36, 38, 56

Badu, Erykah, 13–14, 16, 18
Biden, Joe, 25, 43, 46–47
Black Lives Matter (BLM), 15–16
Black Twitter, 15
Brown, Michael, 16–17, 36

cancel culture, 6, 49–51
Center for American Progress, 36
Chapelle, Dave, 51
Chauvin, Derek, 21
Civil Rights Act, 12, 39
Civil War, 13, 20
Crenshaw, Kimberlé, 27–28, 40
Critical Race Theory (CRT), 6, 38–45
Cruz, Ted, 36

DeGeneres, Ellen, 51
DeSantis, Ron, 32–33, 37–38, 45, 55
Dillion, Seth, 48
discrimination, 12, 23, 29, 34, 36, 38–40, 45, 55–56
Diversity, Equity, and Inclusion (DEI), 29–30

Equality Florida, 45

Federalist Society, 53
Floyd, George, 20–22, 35, 38, 43, 56
French, David, 37

Garvey, Marcus, 9, 12–13, 17
generational wealth, 23

Hannah-Jones, Nikole, 24–26

intersectionality, 27–29, 37

Kendi, Ibram X., 40
King, Martin Luther Jr., 13, 43
Kirk, Charlie, 47–48

Last Poets, 13
Ledbetter, Huddie "Lead Belly," 11, 13
Levine, Rachel, 46–48
LGBTQ+, 27, 29–30, 36, 38, 45, 46, 55
Lizzo, 4–7

Madison, James, 4, 6–7
Malcolm X, 12
Martin, Trayvon, 15
"Master Teacher," 13–14
Miles-Hercules, Deandre, 11–12

Noonan, Peggy, 18

Obama, Barack, 8

Parental Rights Bill, 37, 55
Patrick, Dan, 44–45
pejoration, 17
political correctness, 49

Reconstruction Era, 13
reparations, 23
reverse discrimination, 34
Rowling, J. K., 51
Rubio, Marco, 38
Rufo, Christopher, 39

school curriculum, 26, 38, 43–45
"Scottsboro Boys," 11
segregation, 23, 39, 50, 56
1776 Commission, 25
"1619 Project, The" 24–26
slavery, 6, 20, 22–26, 35
Stop WOKE Act, 45

Trevor Project, 38
Trump, Donald, 17, 25, 34, 39, 41–43, 49
Twitter, 15–16, 34, 47–48, 53

Walt Disney World, 49, 55–56
white privilege, 6, 40, 42
woke capital, 53
"Women of the Year," 47
Women's March, 17
Wood, Peter, 26

Zimmerman, George, 15

IMAGE CREDITS

Cover: © overtheseas/Shutterstock Images
5: © Shawn Miller/LOC Photo/Alamy Live News/Alamy
7: © P. Kijsanayothin/iStockphoto
9: © Evan El-Amin/Shutterstock Images
10: © Everett Collection Inc/Alamy
12: © AP Images
14: © Joseph Sohm/Shutterstock Images
19: © Phil Pasquini/Shutterstock Images
21: © Fiora Watts/Shutterstock Images
24: © Richard Shotwell/Invision/AP Images
28: © Alessandro Biascioli/Shutterstock Images
31: © Jacob Lund/Shutterstock Images
33: © Marta Lavandier/AP Images
35: © Photo Spirit/Shutterstock Images
41: © Evan El-Amin/Shutterstock Images
42: © Drazen Zigic/Shutterstock Images
44: © Evelyn Hockstein/Reuters/Alamy
47: © Wilfredo Lee/AP Images
48: © Jirapong Manustrong/Shutterstock Images
52: © Red Line Editorial
55: © Jerome Labouyrie/Shutterstock Images
57: © pixelfit/iStockphoto
Back Cover: © overtheseas/Shutterstock Images

ABOUT THE AUTHOR

Kate Conley has been writing nonfiction books for children for more than ten years. When she's not writing, Conley spends her time reading, sewing, and solving crossword puzzles. She lives in Minnesota with her husband and two children.